Where Do Plants Grow?

By Lynn Bryan

desert

pond

field

ocean

Plants grow in many places
on the Earth.

Cactuses grow in **deserts**.

Ferns grow in **forests**.

Waterlilies grow in **ponds.**

Potatoes grow in **fields**.

Seaweed grows in **oceans.**

Glossary

 **deserts**   places that get little rain

 **fields**   wide, flat places with few trees

 **forests**   places with many trees

 **oceans**   places with deep, salty water

 **ponds**   places with shallow water